KICK, JUMP, CHEER!
CHEERLEADING COMPETITIONS

BY SARA GREEN

BELLWETHER MEDIA • MINNEAPOLIS, MN

Jump into the cockpit and take flight with Pilot Books. Your journey will take you on high-energy adventures as you learn about all that is wild, weird, fascinating, and fun!

Library of Congress Cataloging-in-Publication Data
Green, Sara, 1964–.
 Cheerleading competitions / by Sara Green.
   p. cm. — (Pilot books: kick, jump, cheer!)
 Includes bibliographical references and index.
 Summary: "Engaging images accompany information about cheerleading competitions. The combination of high-interest subject matter and narrative text is intended for students in grades 3 through 7"
—Provided by publisher.
 ISBN 978-1-60014-648-0 (hardcover : alk. paper)
 1. Cheerleading—Juvenile literature. I. Title.
 LB3635.G743 2011
 791.6'4—dc22   2011010381

Printed in the United States of America, North Mankato, MN.

080111   1187

CONTENTS

PUMPED TO COMPETE

Music pumps through the gym as people take their seats. Excitement is in the air. The judges signal that it's time for the competition to begin. A **squad** of cheerleaders runs onto the floor. For the next few minutes, all eyes will be on them while they perform their **routine**. Will this squad be the winner? This is competitive cheerleading, one of the fastest-growing sports in the United States. Competitive cheerleaders do not cheer for athletes at sporting events. They are the athletes!

Competitive cheerleaders practice after school and often on weekends. Their routines include difficult **stunts**, jumps, and **tumbling**. Most competitive cheerleaders jazz up routines with **choreography**. All the hours of practice pay off when a squad wins a competition.

THE BIRTH OF A SPORT

Cheerleaders have been supporting sports teams for over 100 years. However, the earliest cheerleading competitions did not begin until the 1960s. In 1967, the International Cheerleading Foundation chose the top ten college cheerleading squads. This was the start of competitive cheerleading. In 1978, a competition was shown on television. This allowed many people to see the sport for the first time. By the late 1980s, girls and boys of all ages were participating in competitive cheerleading. Cheerleaders began learning more difficult skills. Advanced tumbling and stunts became common in routines. Competitive cheerleaders proved they were as strong and fit as other athletes. Today, there are competitions across the United States for cheerleaders of almost every age and skill level.

The 2000 movie *Bring It On* is about rival cheerleading squads. It introduced many people to competitive cheerleading and helped increase the sport's popularity.

COMPETING FOR SCHOOL VICTORY

Are you on a school cheerleading squad? Middle school, high school, and college squads compete in local, regional, and national competitions. The competition season starts in the winter and ends in the spring. Local and regional competitions are often held in school gyms. Local competitions are small. Only nearby squads participate.

Regional competitions are larger. They usually include squads from neighboring states. The largest competitions are at the national level. These are held in large cities across the country. The top national competition is held every spring at Disney World in Orlando, Florida. Only the best school squads in the country compete in this exciting event!

ALL-STAR ATHLETES

Many of the top competitive cheerleaders are on All-Star squads. These squads are not part of schools. They practice year-round to prepare for local, state, and national competitions. The top squads compete in world championships. All-Stars practice in special cheerleading gyms that have mats, trampolines, and other equipment. Many of these gyms have mirrors on the walls so cheerleaders can watch themselves in action!

ALL-STAR DIVISIONS
Tiny: 5 years old and younger
Mini: 6 to 8 years old
Youth: 9 to 11 years old
Junior: 12 to 14 years old
Senior: 15 to 18 years old
Open: 18 years old and older

Cheerleaders of all ages can join All-Star squads. Before joining a squad, cheerleaders go through a **tryout**. Coaches place cheerleaders on squads based on their age and skill level. All-Star cheerleading has six divisions. Cheerleaders move up to higher divisions as they get older and their skills improve.

PREPARING FOR COMPETITIONS

Competitive cheerleaders need strong, healthy bodies to perform at their best. Exercise programs help cheerleaders build **stamina**, strength, and **flexibility**. Many cheerleaders join gyms. They work out on their own or in groups. Exercising with friends can help **motivate** you. It also makes fitness more fun! Jogging, swimming, dancing, and jumping rope are great activities that improve stamina. Doing sit-ups and push-ups are simple ways to strengthen muscles. You can increase your flexibility if you stretch before and after you exercise. This also prevents injuries. Coaches can teach cheerleaders safe, easy ways to stretch muscles.

Eating right and getting plenty of rest also help cheerleaders stay in top form. A healthy diet provides fuel for practice and competition. A good night's sleep helps keep energy levels high.

Stunts are an important part of many competitive routines. Each cheerleader has an important role in performing stunts. Coaches choose cheerleaders for roles that fit their physical abilities. **Bases** keep their feet on the floor at all times. They must be steady and strong. Bases lift, throw, and catch cheerleaders called **flyers**. The flyers are often the smallest cheerleaders on the squad. They are lifted high above the others. Flyers should not be afraid of heights! **Spotters** keep the flyers safe. They are alert and ready to catch the flyers if they fall. **Tumblers** perform cartwheels, handsprings, and other moves in front of the others. Stunts look amazing when the squad works together!

In 2003, a squad from the California School for the Deaf was the first deaf cheerleading squad to compete in the International Spirit Championships. They performed their routine to visual cues. They placed first in their division!

IN THE COMPETITION SPOTLIGHT

At a competition, each squad performs a routine set to music. Judges award points for skills, spirit, and **showmanship**. Squads that are able to **rally** the crowd often get more spirit points. Squads perform their most difficult moves at the beginning when they have the most energy. A dance and a **cheer** come in the middle. Squads end routines with an eye-catching **formation**. This big finish must be impressive. It is the last impression they will make on the judges. After every squad has performed, the judges total their points. The highest-scoring squads win awards!

Judges generally award points for the following elements of a routine:
- Jumps and stunts
- Spirit
- Difficulty
- Choreography
- Creativity
- Overall effect

Squads must know the rules for each competition. Most competitions have the same basic rules. One rule is that cheerleaders must have passing grades in school to compete. A second rule is that bases must keep their feet on the ground at all times when they lift and support flyers. This helps them keep their balance. A third rule is that cheerleaders cannot wear any jewelry or glitter. Jewelry can get caught in hair or clothing, and glitter can get into the eyes. Most competitions have rules about stunts and tumbling that are meant to prevent injuries. When everyone follows the rules, competitions stay safe.

Cheerleading squads often raise money so that they can go to competitions. They hold bake sales, car washes, and other fundraising events.

COMMITTED TO WINNING

Are you ready to join a competitive cheerleading squad? To learn more, attend competitions in your area. You will get a feel for the skills you should develop. Once you've made the decision to try out, practice your cheerleading moves. Keep them clean and sharp. Begin working on your strength, flexibility, and stamina. When you're ready, ask your school or All-Star coach for the tryout schedule. At your tryout, show the coaches your skills with confidence. Remember to smile!

Being a competitive cheerleader takes spirit, athletic ability, and commitment. Many squads practice four to seven days a week during competition season. Cheerleaders often attend dance classes, gymnastics classes, and cheerleading camps in their free time. If you love to compete, cheer, and work hard, competitive cheerleading might be the perfect sport for you!

GLOSSARY

bases—cheerleaders who lift and support flyers; bases keep their feet on the ground at all times during a stunt.

cheer—a long phrase yelled in the middle of a routine; jumps and stunts often go along with a cheer.

choreography—steps, patterns, and movements in a routine

flexibility—the ability to stretch and move the body with ease

flyers—cheerleaders who stand on the bases and jump or are tossed into the air

formation—an arrangement of people in a certain shape

motivate—to encourage to do something

rally—to stir up and encourage enthusiasm

routine—a sequence of moves that cheerleaders practice and perform

showmanship—the ability to present something in an exciting, engaging way

spotters—cheerleaders who are ready to help the bases catch the flyers

squad—a group of cheerleaders that works together as a team

stamina—the ability to do something for a long time

stunts—cheerleading moves that involve climbing and lifting; in some stunts cheerleaders are thrown into the air.

tryout—an event where people perform skills for coaches in order to make a team

tumblers—cheerleaders who perform gymnastics moves to add visual excitement to routines

tumbling—gymnastics skills such as cartwheels and handsprings; many cheerleading squads use tumbling in their routines.

TO LEARN MORE

At the Library

Jones, Jen. *Cheer All-Stars: Best of the Best.*
Mankato, Minn.: Capstone Press, 2008.

Maurer, Tracy. *Competitive Cheerleading.*
Vero Beach, Fla.: Rourke Pub., 2006.

Peters, Craig. *Competitive Cheerleading.*
Philadelphia, Pa.: Mason Crest Publishers, 2003.

On the Web

Learning more about cheerleading
is as easy as 1, 2, 3.

1. Go to www.factsurfer.com.

2. Enter "cheerleading" into the search box.

3. Click the "Surf" button and you will see a list of related
    Web sites.

With factsurfer.com, finding more
information is just a click away.

INDEX

The images in this book are reproduced through the courtesy of: Image Source/Getty Images, front cover; Mike Orazzi/The Bristol Press, pp. 5, 8-9, 15, 17, 21; Sports Illustrated/Getty Images, p. 7; Image Source/Photolibrary, pp. 10-11; Plush Studios/Getty Images, p. 13; Alan Edwards/Alamy, p. 19.